This book is dedicated to my wonderful grandma, Mary and selfless mum, Gwen.

First edition February 2021

Self-published by Alex Winstanley
Written by Alex Winstanley
Illustrations & Font copyright © 2021 by Adam Walker-Parker
Edited by Paula Boyd-Rugen

ISBN Paperback: 9798582240631

First printed in the United Kingdom, 2021

My Grandma Has Dementia

Written by Alex Winstanley

Illustrated by Adam Walker-Parker

My grandma has dementia,
but what does that word mean?

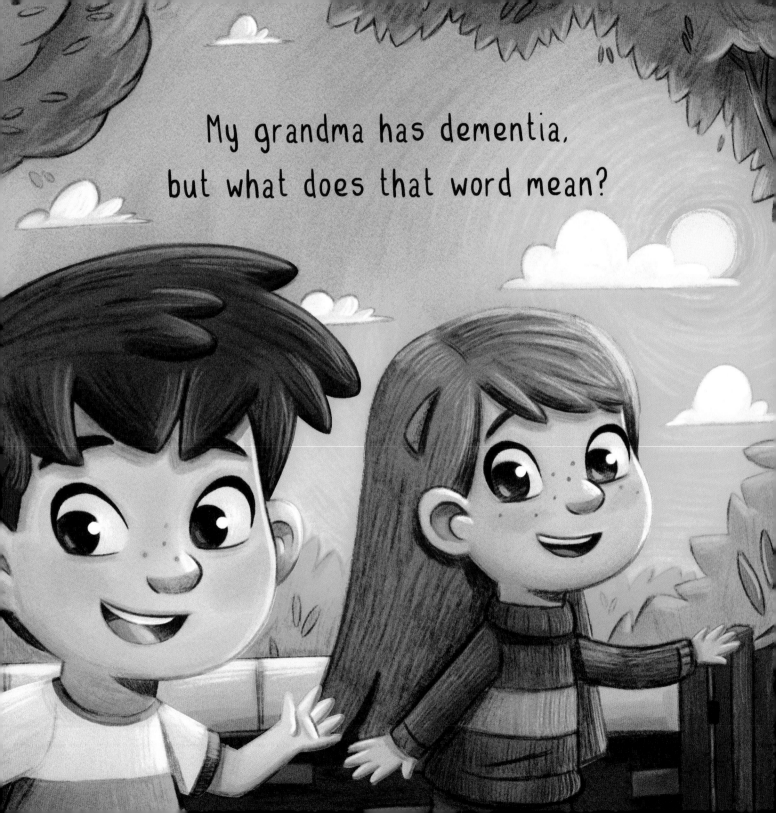

let's talk it through together.
Come along; I'll set the scene.

I loved days at my grandma's,
baking cakes with a smile.

We would listen to her tales,
that would often last a while.

Then we started to notice,
that Grandma forgot each day.

So we went to the doctor,
to see what she had to say.

"It's dementia," said the doctor.
That word made me feel scared.

She explained it very clearly,
so that we felt prepared.

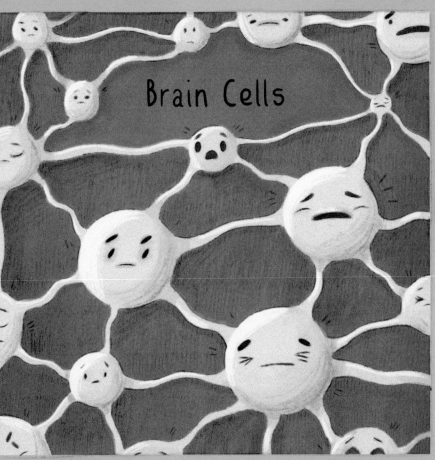

"The cells inside Grandma's brain,
will struggle to work as well.

Medicine can slow this down.
By how much, it's hard to tell."

There are many types of dementia:
Alzheimer's being just one.
It mostly happens to older people,
but *not* to everyone.

Dementia changed a lot of things:
the way Grandma thought and talked.

It sometimes changed the way she felt and even how she walked.

Grandma would often wonder
about who and why or where.

We reminded her to eat and drink
and even to brush her hair.

"I'm befuddled!" Grandma would say,
which meant she felt confused.
We knew to be patient and clear
with the words that we used.

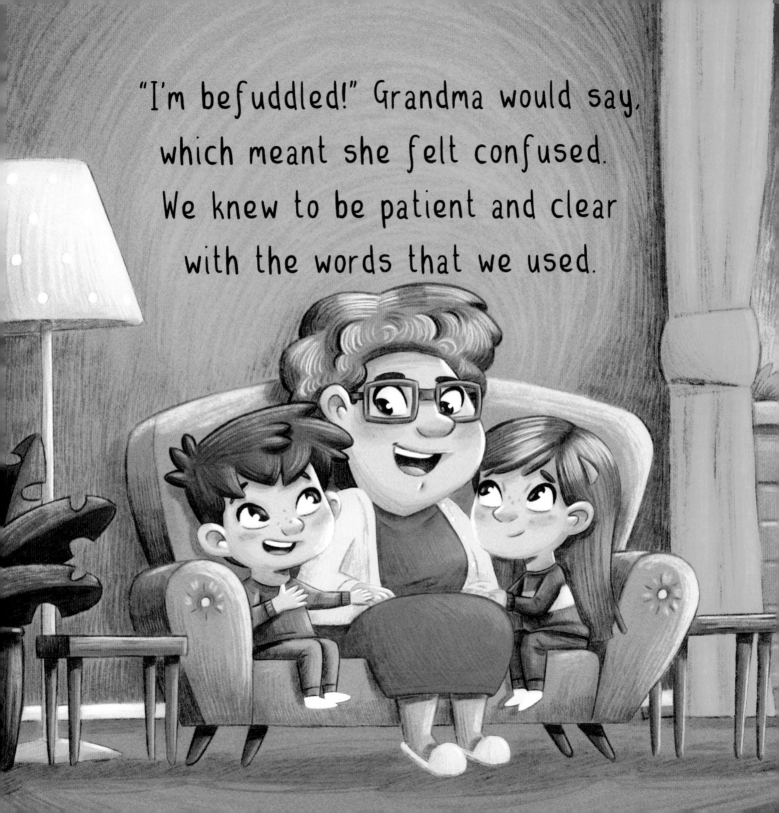

We left notes around her house
about what to do and when.
We tried to make more space,
though she still fell now and then.

To make sure Grandma was okay,
she moved to a safer place.
At the care home where we visit,
there's always a friendly face.

Grandma plays lots of games,
keeping busy all the while.

Dementia will never go away,
but neither will her smile!

My grandma has dementia.
Now you know about it too.

When you meet someone with dementia,
you'll know just what to do.

Support Information

Happy Smiles Training
Creating Inclusive Communities

 /happysmilestrainingcic

 @happysmilescic

 @happysmilestrainingcic

Happy Smiles Training CIC was initially created as a blog, inspired by a young man with complex needs who always has a smile on his face!

We empower disabled young adults to deliver training across schools, community groups, businesses and more. Our aim is to creative inclusive communities and 100% of our organisation is made up of people with lived experience of disability.

Call - 07917221503
Email - info@happysmilestraining.co.uk
Website - www.happysmilestraining.co.uk

In aid of

Alzheimer's Society
United Against Dementia

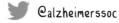 /alzheimerssocietyuk

@alzheimerssoc

@alzheimerssoc

We know dementia affects everyone differently. So whether you, a loved one, a friend or neighbour is affected by dementia, we're here to support you.

Dementia Connect, Alzheimer's Society's personalised support service, means you're only one click or call away from the dementia support you need.

It's free, easy to access, and puts you in touch with the right support, from local help to phone and online advice. Helping make things easier.

Call - 0333 150 3456
Website - www.alzheimers.org.uk/dementiaconnect
Website - www.alzheimers.org.uk

www.theabilitiesinme.com

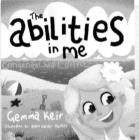

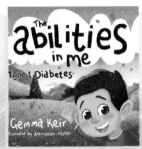

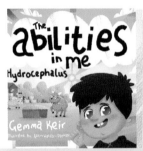
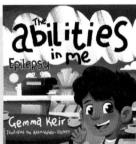

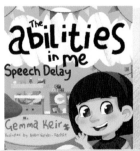
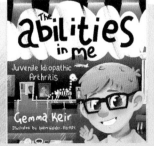
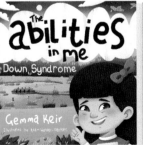

About the Author

My name is Alex Winstanley. I am an author, teacher and social entrepreneur from Wigan, England. My background as a teacher, as well as a carer to young disabled adults, has shaped my outlook on the inclusion of disabled people and those with long-term health conditions, across society. Through my books, I aim to raise awareness of a range of long-term health conditions, in a positive and supportive way, for children and young people. I am extremely passionate about promoting a diverse and inclusive society, in which every person is valued and celebrated. Each one of my books is inspired by real people, as I believe there is nothing more important than giving a voice to those with lived experience.

www.instagram.com/alexwinstanleyauthor
www.facebook.com/alexwinstanleyauthor
www.twitter.com/alexwauthor

About the Illustrator

My name is Adam Walker-Parker. I am an artist and illustrator represented by lemonade Illustration Agency from the Cairngorm National Park in the Highlands of Scotland. I focus on creating illustrations for books that are fun and engaging and that help to raise awareness of many health conditions. I enjoy creating images with inclusion and diversity in mind.

www.awalkerparker.com

In loving memory of Mary Perry
22nd March 1933 - 23rd December 2020

Goodnight, God bless

To a loving mum and grandma,
An auntie, sister and more.
We've rarely felt more loved,
Than after walking through your door.

Any time with you Grandma,
Was filled with love and laughter.
As kids, we'd tip your house upside down,
Then sleep through your snoring after.

Like your daughter, you cared for many,
With the most beautiful smile.
Even running around after us,
You would be smiling, all the while.

"This is little Reg & little Mary,"
You'd proudly say, to anyone who'd allow.
Always followed by my mum asking,
"Who's she talking to now?"

Befuddled over the years,
Some memories might fade.
But your love always stayed strong,
Because of the bond we had made.

"Eh I do love you," you'd tell us,
We knew just how much that was meant.
And we'll be forever grateful,
For all the time together, we spent.

"I wish your grandad was here,"
You would often say to me.
"You'd get on like a house on fire,"
You'd say, and I would always agree.

But I've always believed he's around,
And I know that you will be too.
Reminding us to enjoy and take care,
In everything that we do.

So, thank you for everything Grandma,
It's now your turn to get some rest.
We'll be together again one day,
For now, goodnight, god bless.

By Alex Winstanley